HANNAH MOSCOVITCH

Hannah Moscovitch is one of Canada's most prominent playwrights. She has written sixteen plays, including *East of Berlin*, *Sexual Misconduct of the Middle Classes* and *This is War*, and she has been honoured with numerous awards, among them the Governor General's Literary Award, the Nova Scotia MasterWorks Arts Award, and the prestigious Windham-Campbell Prize. Hannah's music-theatre hybrid *Old Stock: A Refugee Love Story* (co-created with Christian Barry and Ben Caplan) became a *Time Out* and *New York Times* Critic's Pick, winning Herald Angel and Scotsman Fringe First Awards at the Edinburgh Festival Fringe, and receiving six Drama Desk Award nominations in New York, crossing the 400-performance line in the process. In television, Hannah is Co-Creator, Executive Producer, and Head Writer of *Little Bird* alongside showrunner Jennifer Podemski, which has garnered a landslide of awards and critical praise, including the Séries Maria Prix Public (or Audience Award) and thirteen Canadian Screen Awards, including Best Drama Series. Most recently, Hannah was Co-Executive Producer on Season One and Season Two of AMC's hit series *Interview with the Vampire*.

Other Titles in this Series

Waleed Akhtar
THE ART OF ILLUSION *after* Alexis Michalik
KABUL GOES POP: MUSIC TELEVISION
  AFGHANISTAN
THE P WORD
THE REAL ONES

Chris Bush
THE ASSASSINATION OF KATIE HOPKINS
  with Matt Winkworth
THE CHANGING ROOM
CHRIS BUSH PLAYS: ONE
A DOLL'S HOUSE *after* Ibsen
FAUSTUS: THAT DAMNED WOMAN
HUNGRY
JANE EYRE *after* Brontë
THE LAST NOËL
OTHERLAND
ROBIN HOOD AND THE CHRISTMAS HEIST
  with Matt Winkworth
ROCK / PAPER / SCISSORS
STANDING AT THE SKY'S EDGE
  with Richard Hawley
STEEL

Jez Butterworth
THE FERRYMAN
THE HILLS OF CALIFORNIA
JERUSALEM
JEZ BUTTERWORTH PLAYS: ONE
JEZ BUTTERWORTH PLAYS: TWO
MOJO
THE NIGHT HERON
PARLOUR SONG
THE RIVER
THE WINTERLING

Caryl Churchill
BLUE HEART
CHURCHILL PLAYS: THREE
CHURCHILL PLAYS: FOUR
CHURCHILL PLAYS: FIVE
CHURCHILL: SHORTS
CLOUD NINE
DING DONG THE WICKED
A DREAM PLAY *after* Strindberg
DRUNK ENOUGH TO SAY I LOVE YOU?
ESCAPED ALONE
FAR AWAY
GLASS. KILL. BLUEBEARD'S FRIENDS. IMP.
HERE WE GO
HOTEL
ICECREAM
LIGHT SHINING IN BUCKINGHAMSHIRE
LOVE AND INFORMATION
MAD FOREST
A NUMBER
PIGS AND DOGS
SEVEN JEWISH CHILDREN
THE SKRIKER
THIS IS A CHAIR
THYESTES *after* Seneca
TRAPS
WHAT IF IF ONLY

Branden Jacobs-Jenkins
APPROPRIATE
THE COMEUPPANCE
GLORIA
AN OCTOROON

Lucy Kirkwood
BEAUTY AND THE BEAST *with* Katie Mitchell
BLOODY WIMMIN
THE CHILDREN
CHIMERICA
HEDDA *after* Ibsen
THE HUMAN BODY
IT FELT EMPTY WHEN THE HEART WENT
  AT FIRST BUT IT IS ALRIGHT NOW
LUCY KIRKWOOD PLAYS: ONE
MOSQUITOES
NSFW
RAPTURE
TINDERBOX
THE WELKIN

Adam Lazarus
DAUGHTER

Suzie Miller
INTER ALIA
PRIMA FACIE

Nina Raine
BACH & SONS
CONSENT
THE DRUNKS
  after Mikhail and Vyacheslav Durnekov
RABBIT STORIES
TIGER COUNTRY
TRIBES

Jack Thorne
2ND MAY 1997
AFTER LIFE *after* Hirokazu Kore-eda
BUNNY
BURYING YOUR BROTHER IN THE
  PAVEMENT
A CHRISTMAS CAROL *after* Dickens
THE END OF HISTORY…
HOPE
FANNY AND FAGGOT
JACK THORNE PLAYS: ONE
JACK THORNE PLAYS: TWO
JUNKYARD
LET THE RIGHT ONE IN
  after John Ajvide Lindqvist
THE MOTIVE AND THE CUE
MYDIDAE
THE SOLID LIFE OF SUGAR WATER
STACY
WHEN WINSTON WENT TO WAR WITH
  THE WIRELESS
WHEN YOU CURE ME
WOYZECK *after* Büchner

debbie tucker green
BORN BAD
DEBBIE TUCKER GREEN PLAYS: ONE
DIRTY BUTTERFLY
EAR FOR EYE
HANG
NUT
A PROFOUNDLY AFFECTIONATE,
  PASSIONATE DEVOTION TO SOMEONE
  (– *NOUN*)
RANDOM
STONING MARY
TRADE & GENERATIONS
TRUTH AND RECONCILIATION

Hannah Moscovitch

RED LIKE FRUIT

NICK HERN BOOKS

London
www.nickhernbooks.co.uk

A Nick Hern Book

Red Like Fruit first published in Great Britain in 2025 as a paperback original by Nick Hern Books Limited, The Glasshouse, 49a Goldhawk Road, London W12 8QP, by special arrangement with Playwrights Canada Press, Toronto

Red Like Fruit copyright © 2025 Hannah Moscovitch

Hannah Moscovitch has asserted her moral right to be identified as the author of this work

Cover photograph of Michelle Monteith by Riley Smith

Designed and typeset by Nick Hern Books, London
Printed and bound in Great Britain by Mimeo Ltd, Huntingdon, Cambridgeshire PE29 6XX

A CIP catalogue record for this book is available from the British Library

ISBN 978 1 83904 502 8

CAUTION All rights whatsoever in this play are strictly reserved. Requests to reproduce the text in whole or in part should be addressed to the publisher. This book may not be used, in whole or in part, for the development or training of artificial intelligence technologies or systems.

Applications for performance, including readings and excerpts, throughout the world should be addressed to Colin Rivers at Marquis Literary, *web* MQlit.ca *email* colin@mqent.ca

No performance of any kind may be given unless a licence has been obtained. Applications should be made before rehearsals begin. Publication of this play does not necessarily indicate its availability for performance.

www.nickhernbooks.co.uk/environmental-policy

Nick Hern Books' authorised representative in the EU is
Easy Access System Europe – Mustamäe tee 50, 10621 Tallinn, Estonia
email gpsr.requests@easproject.com

To Christian Barry

Red Like Fruit was first produced by 2b theatre company at the Bus Stop Theatre, Halifax, on 3 April 2024. The cast was as follows:

LAUREN	Michelle Monteith
LUKE	David Patrick Flemming
Director	Christian Barry
Designer	Kaitlin Hickey
Stage Manager	Don Brownrigg
Production Manager	Sylvia Bell
Accessibility Coordinator	Sara Graham

It transferred to the Traverse Theatre for the Edinburgh Festival Fringe on 31 July 2025. The cast was as follows:

LAUREN	Michelle Monteith
LUKE	David Patrick Flemming
Director	Christian Barry
Designer	Kaitlin Hickey
Stage Manager	Alison Crosby
Company Manager	Olivia Rankin

Characters

LAUREN, *in her early forties*
LUKE

Notes

What Lauren is doing while Luke speaks is up to the director. It could be abstract. It could be choreography. It could be some version of nothing. Lauren, though, listens to Luke and watches the audience. That's her main thing. Luke's main thing is inhabiting Lauren's voice.

This text went to press before the end of rehearsals and so may differ slightly from the play as performed.

Prologue

LAUREN. Hi.
　I'm Lauren.
　This is Luke.

LUKE. Hi.

LAUREN. I've asked Luke to speak for me.

　LAUREN *sits and* LUKE *remains standing.*

　LUKE *looks at* LAUREN.

LUKE (*to* LAUREN). Yeah?

LAUREN (*to* LUKE). Yeah.

LUKE. Okay.

　Let's start.

　Shift.

Start.

LUKE. Lauren buys a coffee
   Crosses the street
   And goes into CAMH
   Which is
   A mental hospital
   In Toronto.
   She goes down the long corridor
   Finds the room
   Looks around at the other women and feels deeply, deeply uncool.
   She thinks mostly it's women who do this in groups
   Isn't it?
   Talk about their problems?
   Their daddy hang-ups
   Their shitty exes
   And how they can't move on.
   Men click on porn
   Go fishing
   Get loaded
   Cry into each other's shirts
   Pretend they didn't?
   The session hasn't started so Lauren spends the first few minutes trying to solve shit on her phone
   Set up interviews for an article she's been assigned (a high-profile case of domestic violence)
   Which counteracts her feeling of uncoolness and distracts her from
   The drab room and the overweight women.
   The psychologist comes in
   And Lauren wonders if he can
   Help her?
   He explains the hopes and anticipated outcomes and how untwisting your thinking is the optimal whatever.

The psychologist
Asks them each to say why they're in group.
There's a thoughtful silence.
Lauren is surprised
She finds she likes
That none of the women laugh or roll their eyes.
One of them
A woman named Alice
Says that after her husband left her
She regretted keeping the house so cold
Maybe if she'd kept it two degrees warmer he would've
stayed and not had sex with his assistant curator.
Lauren looks at the floor.
She can't help but think
But what if some men do just want a woman who's
A pretty object to have in the room
And companionship only comes when he's with other
businessmen?
What in the end is the point of getting angry about that if
that's what some men want?
Then Alice the woman left by her husband
Says cautiously
That she doesn't think it was the temperature of her house.
Not really.
All along the problem was that her husband wanted a woman
to look up to him
Instead of one who looked directly at him
Which makes Lauren like Alice
Because she says it thoughtfully and without self-pity.
When it's Lauren's turn she says
'I'm not sure what's wrong with me.'

Beat.

Half of Lauren's friends have a kid with autism or cerebral
palsy or
They have nothing in their bank accounts in case of cancer.
Her husband's good
Her children are good
She has

Disposable income.
Aren't those all the preconditions for joy?
There isn't anything obviously wrong with her other than this vague sense of
Unease
That's been escalating over the last few months.
The women look at her
Thinking through what she's said.
Lauren likes this too
That they're considering her attentively.
One of them says
'There might be things that don't make sense but that are real.'
And another woman says
'It's okay if it's small things that have piled up into a big pile.'
And that's when the psychologist intervenes
'I want to remind you all not to offer advice.'
And Lauren
Who has been appreciating the advice
Thinks
'Huh.'
'Huh.'
'I'm angry.'
And
'Maybe I should tell someone I get angry and I don't know why.'
And anyway why be angry?
This psychologist's probably right that advice from these women who aren't professionals could be unhelpful.

Shift.

When the session ends
Lauren goes home
Kisses her husband
(He's on his way to pick up a client from the airport and take them to a baseball game to 'build rapport'.)
Sits down in her home office
To work on the article about domestic violence.

An employee
Of the Liberal Party
In a top position
Was charged with assaulting his long-term girlfriend.
He pled guilty and was sentenced to community work
And then he'd been rehired at his old job
And somehow it was all hushed up and is only now hitting the news
Which seems almost impossible
Like how did this slip through the cracks?
The man's name is *Andrew*
Lauren thinks.
It feels improbable that anyone named Andrew who has a good track record on climate change beats his wife.

Shift.

Lauren calls Andrew's boss
Justin the MP.
When the phone picks up
The man on the line says
'Is this about the slap?'
And Lauren thinks
'Oh okay'
'A slap.'
She has no problem imagining herself losing her temper and wanting to if not going through with a slap.
As they make pleasant opening comments Justin sounds
Assured.
That steady authority of a man who has been listened to often
Friendly enough within the parameters of a political operative.
Lauren asks
Neutrally
How Justin became aware of the incident?
Justin says Andrew came into the office the next day pale and 'off' and told him there had been a bad situation with Brittany.
Only later did Justin understand police were involved

That it was a criminal matter.
Justin's answer sounds rehearsed
A more polished version of the truth arrived at through repetition and that's fine
Lauren expected that.
Lauren asks
'And what were Andrew and Brittany like to work with?'
And here Justin hesitates.
She hears his mental manoeuvring.
Lauren takes her hands off her laptop keys and waits.
When Justin speaks
His tone suggests that
It's uncomfortable to be in a position of conveying an unsavoury truth that doesn't align with his political values.
Justin says
'Brittany had a tendency toward attention-seeking behaviour.'
She had
As far as he knows
Reasons for her behavioural issues
And here there's an implication that there are traumas in Brittany's childhood that can't be mentioned or that the whole of Brittany's childhood was a trauma
And it's horrible to say
And no one wants it to be the case
But that is how Brittany was.
There's also a slight implication in Justin's tone that Andrew is one of these men who picks vacuous volatile women.
There's a pause and then
Lauren asks
'Andrew hit her?'
Justin doesn't hesitate at all now.
Yes
Andrew slapped her.
He did
Yes.
Lauren says mildly
I have two children
I tell them 'Don't hit.'

Lauren can sense that Justin smiles indulgently.
He says
'Yes, agreed.'
'Andrew shouldn't have hit her.'
But there's something in his tone that suggests Justin would have liked to hit Brittany himself
And that Brittany almost wanted to be hit so she could garner the sympathy or attention or attention in the form of sympathy she was so desperate for.
And also something in Justin's tone
That suggests that of course Brittany is going to do what Brittanies in these circumstances do
Which is make herself the centre of attention
And Brittany is both dangerous and pitiable.
Lauren asks
'You hired Andrew back?'
On the other end of the line Justin seems to be nodding.
Justin's tone has an apology in it
Yes it would've been better for them not to rehire Andrew from an ethical and also an optical standpoint
But Andrew's work as an organiser within the party is critical
And Andrew had gone through the judicial process and been penalised and rehabilitated and it was the hope of the Liberal Party that the Canadian judicial system works.
Lauren asks
'And where is Brittany employed now?'
And here there's an intake of breath
And a rueful tone that implies that
Yes
Lauren has done her job and caught Justin out.
Yes.
'Good point.'
Yes
Brittany's role was less senior and her contract wasn't renewed.
At this juncture in the interview Justin pauses and tells Lauren he read a couple of her articles ahead of this interview and she's a very good journalist.

The implication is that Justin knows or trusts that Lauren won't stoop to sensationalism.
His voice is steady
Confident.
The compliment rings true.
And this Lauren supposes is
Charm?
The call concludes with Justin calmly offering further help.
Yes they want to be transparent with her
And yes they knew the media might have
And here his tone implies
'Very valid' questions about why they are continuing to employ Andrew.
Lauren nods and nods and then hangs up the phone.
She sits at her desk
Head tilted to one side.
Lauren realises she wanted Justin to like her
Which is
Unsettling.

Beat.

Then Lauren rouses herself and dials this woman who was slapped by her ex-boyfriend.
The phone rings a number of times before the woman picks up.
She sounds
Neutral on the phone
Cautious.
Lauren asks her what happened.
The woman
Named Brittany
Which somehow doesn't help her case
Says
'I lost two teeth.'
And then
'He was on top of me
Punching me
And yeah part of
Part of what

What happened was that after he punched me like that he had uh
Sex
Intercourse with me and I wasn't saying no to the sex exactly but my teeth had been pushed back against the roof of my mouth.'
Lauren at her laptop blinks
Closes her eyes
Clears her throat
Asks
What Brittany thinks about Andrew's version of the story
That it was a slap.
Brittany says quietly
'I don't have any thoughts about that.'
But in Brittany's tone Lauren hears wariness and something else
Is it confusion?
Or tamped-down rage?
Or exhaustion?
A desire to gently put the phone down and walk away?
Lauren asks
'What do you think about Andrew being hired back at his former job?'
Brittany says
'I don't feel great about it.'
Lauren asks
'What do you think about them not hiring you back?'
Brittany says mildly
'I wouldn't have gone back anyway.'
Lauren asks
'Had Andrew ever hit you in the past?'
Brittany says
'Not – no…'
Lauren waits
Lets a pause open up.
Brittany says
'He shoved me during arguments a couple of times.'
Lauren asks
Formally

If she can call back with any further questions that might
arise.
Brittany says 'yes' but there's a sense
As they hang up
That Brittany's hoping not to hear from her again.
And this
Here is where
It doesn't make sense
And Lauren doesn't know why
Aside from the obvious.
The incident Brittany described is disturbing.
(But she's covered worse.)
The uneasiness she's tried to describe to various doctors in
various clinical settings sets in.
This feeling of constriction
Of
As though
She's
Being dragged backward
Toward some
Horrible

LAUREN *closes her eyes for a moment.*

LUKE *turns and regards her.*

To defuse the feeling
Lauren goes on Twitter and clicks and clicks.

LUKE *glances at* LAUREN *again. Her eyes are still closed.*

I'm sorry.

Are

Are you okay?

LAUREN *opens her eyes.*

LAUREN. Oh

    Yeah.
    Yeah.
    Fine.

LUKE. Okay.

Sorry.

Beat.

I'll
Go back to the…?

LAUREN. Yeah.

LUKE *returns to the text.*

LUKE. Next Lauren gets on the phone with the ex-boyfriend
himself
Andrew
And asks for his comment.
She keeps her voice jokey and low
To make herself sound more like a buddy of his.
Andrew says
'I did the wrong thing.
I did
I was charged and I pled guilty.
Now I'm trying to put my life back together.'
He sounds so impossibly normal and reasonable
Like a person who made a singular mistake.
Lauren asks him
'How do you feel about Brittany's injuries?'
Andrew says he slapped her while she was balanced on a
chair in their kitchen and she lost her balance and
She fell backward into a wall.
Lauren asks how it happened.
Andrew pauses and says
'If you've read the police report…
Britanny was drunk.'
When Lauren asks about punching he says 'no'
He slapped her
Open-handed
One time
No punching.
Lauren says
'What about the teeth that were bent back against the roof of

Brittany's mouth and the surgeries to remove those teeth and then to replace those teeth first with dentures on a twenty-seven-year-old woman and then the four or five surgeries for implants over the course of twenty-one months?'
There's a pause
Then Andrew says quietly
'Yeah
It must have been terrible.'
And
'I remember the sound when she hit the wall.'
And then
'I watched her fall backward and immediately I knew how bad it was going to be and and I remember how sick I felt that I had done that to her.'
And then
'It wasn't a good night.'
They talk a little longer about the courses Andrew was required to complete on how not to commit domestic violence and on the other men he met along the way (here it sounds like Andrew made some blue-collar friends) and his community service at a public library and what it was like to return to his job with the Liberal Party and if he was welcomed back or if there was any residual wariness or mistrust (yes many jokes were made in the style of 'don't piss off Andrew').
At the end of the call Andrew says
'I know it'll sound self-serving
But I want you to know I lost it in that moment and I lashed out but I didn't mean for her to sustain that kind of damage to her teeth I really didn't and I've been trying to figure out why I did something that was so obviously wrong and bad.'
Then concluding pleasantries and
Lauren slowly puts down the phone.
She imagines her son as a grown man with the same half-smile as her husband
And he's arguing with a girl
A blonde girl who wears flip-flops and posts a lot of photos of herself at the beach with captions like
'I am soooooo loaded.'

Lauren pictures this girl saying some offhand stupid thing
and then her son
Smacks this girl.
The shocked look on her son's face as the girl stumbles and
one knee twists and touches the ground.
And the call she'd receive from her son
Emotion slurring his voice
'Mom, I lost it, I did something bad.'
And isn't that
Is that
Is it okay to make a mistake?
How much good behaviour can we expect all the time from
all the
Boys?
Men?

LAUREN *exhales and leans forward, holding her head in her hands, her fingers in her hair.* LUKE *turns and looks at her momentarily.*

Lauren
I'm sorry.
Are you good?

LAUREN. Good.

LAUREN, *her head still down, nods.*

Yeah.
Yes.
Just…
We're
Getting into it.

LUKE. Do you want to stop for a sec?

LAUREN. No.

Uh
No
But I am uh
Probably gonna uh
Along the way

It might be…

LUKE. Yeah

Of course.

LAUREN. It's okay.
You can keep going

LUKE *goes back to the text.*

LUKE. Late that night
Lauren lies in bed beside her husband
Listening to the house
Hoping her thoughts will disarticulate into sleep.
The dryer down in the basement is squeaking
And out on the street streetcars are going by
And then
The grey corridors of her mind turn onto an unfamiliar street
Cobblestoned.
She thinks
'Oh it's
Is it
Prague?'
When she was fifteen?
A family holiday in Prague?
Her parents beside her on the cobblestoned street and Lauren
bored and sulky and annoyed to be spending so much time
with her family and her mother lecturing her about her 'lack
of gratitude' and then her father hiring a tour guide to escort
the family around a semi-submerged crypt.
The tour guide with the big moustache who seemed so
warm-hearted.
Once they were down in the crypt
The tour guide was
Helping her to not trip in the darkened underground tunnels
On the uneven rocks
But as he'd helped he'd caught her
Between her legs.

Beat.

And no joke her mother and father and little brother and little sister were no more than ten feet ahead.

She'd tried to speed up in the darkened crypt and put her mother and father between her and the moustached man and she'd fallen and skinned her knee

And her father had said

'Lauren, come on. What are you doing? Don't run in the dark.'

Out in the sunlight she watched the tour guide closely

But no he seemed professional and barely looked at her.

And then

Her mom had said in an upbraiding tone

'Lauren, thank the tour guide.'

And Lauren had

Turned and

Thanked the tour guide

So as not to seem like she lacked gratitude.

What a weird thing to remember and with so little emotion attached to it.

Lauren throws off the duvet and gets up.

She walks down the hallway to her daughter's and son's bedrooms

Stops in their doorways like she's in a movie to watch them sleep.

But unmovie-like she's thinking

What

In the end

Does it matter?

What

In the end

Is the difference between trauma and experience?

Because aren't those small *whatever* things that happen in adolescence just a part of it all?

Beat.

Standing in the hallway outside –

LAUREN. Aren't…

LUKE *looks at* LAUREN.

>   Aren't those things just part of it all?
>   Aren't they?
>
>   *Shift.*
>
>   Sorry to interrupt and
>   Ask you
>   But
>   I can't help but think that.

LUKE. Part of what?

LAUREN. I don't know
>   Growing up?

LUKE. Uh
>   Well
>   Uh
>   I can try
>   To answer that.
>   You want me to?

LAUREN. Yeah.

LUKE. Okay uh
>   The tour guide
>   He was trying to stop you from tripping?

>   LAUREN *nods.*

LAUREN. Yeah he was.

LUKE. And how did he do it?

LAUREN. As I tripped forward on the rocks
>   He caught me but he didn't put his hands on my waist:
>   He uh

LUKE. So you tripped forward and he caught you
>   But as he caught you
>   He caught you by the
>   So you trip and he catches you by the
>   Vagina?

>   LAUREN *nods.*

LUKE *looks at* LAUREN.

LAUREN. Okay yeah.

LUKE. I don't

> I don't
> I think there were better ways for him to stop you from tripping.
> Don't you?
> How could that have helped?
> I don't mean to sound glib and I understand you're asking me a broader question about growing up but I don't
> I'm not sure how to
> Answer the broader question?

LAUREN. No yeah.

LUKE. The simple answer is yeah
> He was using it being dark and you being fifteen and you being scared or embarrassed and staying quiet to
> Put his hands on you.

> LAUREN *gazes at him for a moment, trying to orient herself.*

LAUREN. Yeah.

> *Pause.*

LUKE. I'll go on?

LAUREN. Yeah.

> LUKE *returns to the text.*

LUKE. Standing in the hallway outside her children's rooms
> Lauren turns
> And goes into her home office.
> She fumbles through her handbag
> Finds her phone
> Calls her dad on his cell.
> He's usually up late in his office playing the stock market.
> When he picks up and asks her what's going on
> She says

'I don't know, Dad.
I'm fine I think?'
After a few minutes of small talk with her dad
(Apparently his stock portfolio is doing great!)
Lauren starts to cry.
It's soothing to listen to her dad's exhilaration over making money while she cries silently
Because yes
She's pissed off that she's having these weird thoughts about her childhood and what was okay and what wasn't
And yes
Her father
If he thought about it
Could surmise that if his daughter is calling this late at night then maybe there's something wrong
But what's the point of
Wanting your father to notice something he isn't going to notice?
Lauren hangs up the phone and finds somehow hanging up makes it worse and she puts her head down and cries
But why get
Worked up about it all?

Shift.

The next morning
Once the children have been driven to school and Lauren's walked around the house picking up
The small shirts the breakfast bowls the glittery pieces of confetti all over the floor from an art project
She sits back down at her laptop
Tries to still herself.
Her first interview is with a neighbour of Brittany and Andrew's that she's gotten in touch with by painstakingly reading through the police report
And now
An elderly woman comes on the phone
Named Gladys.

LAUREN *looks up, leaning forward on her elbows.*

Lauren says
'Thank you for your time.'
And Gladys says
'Of course, dear.'
Lauren says
'You heard the fight that night?'
Gladys says yes
Through the walls
Thumping and wailing and
Brittany saying 'let me up' a number of times…
Gladys pauses then and says
'The sound of it wasn't right, like a child or a dog crying.'
Lauren feels herself sit upright
And lean forward.
She asks what Gladys's impressions were of Andrew.
Gladys says
'Oh him?
He's a stone-cold creep.'
And Lauren
Blinks
And blinks
And says
'You didn't say that to the police.'
And Gladys says no
They asked her questions about what happened
They didn't ask her to characterise either Brittany or Andrew.
And immediately Lauren realises how stupid she sounds
As though she hasn't covered cases like this one before
Of course you don't characterise
You just answer the questions the police ask you.

Shift.

The next call is to the ER resident who saw Brittany that night.
His name is Doctor Daniel Kim and he gets on a Zoom call from his office at the hospital.
Right away Lauren thinks he has a good professional manner.

Even though he looks young there's something about him that strikes her as impartial.
Doctor Kim tells her in a curt tone that he advised Brittany not to waive her doctor–patient confidentiality for a magazine article.
The implication being that Brittany is too vulnerable – or possibly too reckless? – to look after herself.
Lauren goes over what Andrew told her about the incident.
Doctor Kim listens to her carefully
Impassively
Then he tells her without hesitation that when he saw Brittany
She looked like a car-accident victim
Because of the severity of the injuries
Teeth pushed back
Lacerations
And the amount of blood from the head wound.
Doctor Kim says Brittany was silent when she came in in the ambulance accompanied by police
Silent but conscious.
He found that worrying.
Lauren at that moment catches sight of herself in the Zoom window and sees she's grimacing.
Lauren asks if the type of abrasions on Brittany's face and arms were consistent with a slap and falling into a wall?
Doctor Kim considers the question coolly then says that he doesn't have the expertise to assess that.
That would be a question for the police.
Lauren asks if there's anything Doctor Kim would like to add.
He thinks for a moment
Looking down
Then he says
'Yeah I'd like to add: don't beat up women.'

Shift.

The detachment Lauren feels turns into

Something

Else that is
So big and pit-like.

LAUREN *looks down.*

Shift.

Lauren dials the number for her final interview of the day

With Brittany's mother
Who
Sounds sensible
No-nonsense
If a little reluctant to speak about 'this whole thing' again.
The mother
Whose name is Judy
And who works as an administrator at a hospital
Says
Brittany is
Her daughter of course
But
Brittany has had a tendency that they all hoped she'd grow out of toward
Not lying but exaggeration
And that Brittany 'is a drinker' and a bit of a 'chaos agent'
And yes of course Andrew hit her
Which makes him a jackass
But somehow Brittany
Is very good at 'playing the victim' when the need arises.
Brittany was diagnosed with borderline personality disorder
And Judy wouldn't be surprised if these type of things keep happening in her daughter's life.
Judy admits to Lauren
She'd liked Andrew
Because he seemed so stable until
What happened happened.
Lauren asks carefully about what Brittany's childhood was like
And
Judy says
'I have two daughters and one of them is just fine

And the other one is
Brittany.'
And after more of this
Of Judy's brittle admissions that there's something wrong
with her daughter
Lauren hangs up the phone and closes the lid of her laptop.
She gets up stiffly
Thinks to herself
'That's enough
I can't think about this any more.'

LAUREN *takes out a tube of lipstick and applies it.*

She finds a tube of lipstick

Smears it on
A bright
Orange-red
Checks her emails on her phone to make sure her children
are okay
Grabs her handbag
And heads out.
A lunch with a colleague.

Shift.

The restaurant is a good one and she's looking forward to the
quality of the food

The quality of the conversation she'll have with this
colleague.
The colleague is a couple of minutes late.
Lauren orders a glass of wine
And enjoys the thoughts that flick through her mind.
That it's good to be her age.
The age where you can sit in a restaurant by yourself
Sipping a glass of wine
Looking out at the world
Blunted
With a sense of humour about it all.
The confusion of being young and having no clear love

No clear career
No clear life turned down.
Lauren's colleague shows up.
As he takes off his coat and scarf he's already talking about the pall that's fallen in the wake of the MeToo movement
Over the journalism department where he's an associate professor.
He tells her in quick broken phrases
That he's
(The waitress takes their order but it doesn't break his flow.)
He's thinking about the men he knows
And speculating about which of them
If any
Like to get their dick out at work
Corner women in their offices
Hit on them when all the cues point to 'fuck off'.
These men
Who must somehow conclude that a woman
Blonde
An intern
Or a student
Only twenty-one years old
Could be very hot for a man with greying hair and a puffy gut and diminishing sex appeal.
While Lauren sips her white wine
Lauren's colleague is saying
That he's not sure he gets on an animal level
What the whole 'getting your dick out to just show it to someone' is all about
Or putting your phone down your pants and clicking.
What's the gratification of knowing your dick is out there on someone else's phone?
Just dick in the wind
But all around him men are falling like suicides off buildings so there must be a set of unsavoury predilections that he's personally unfamiliar with or hopes he is.
Lauren looks at her colleague
And his mouth moving and moving.
She could say to him

Yes she too feels unsettled these days
She too feels as though the world's tilted sideways
But instead she listens
And listens
Until
In her mind
A bathtub
A bathtub filled with blood

Shift.

Lauren's colleague's still going on and on with obvious personal discomfort about the MeToo movement.
It crosses Lauren's mind that
In all this time of her colleague monologuing
In forty-five minutes of him monologuing and her un-huhing it hasn't occurred to him that she is
A woman and might have
Thoughts
About the MeToo movement.
And with that thought comes fucked-up feelings
And sudden-onset rage
Like she'd like to punch her colleague in the mouth
This long-time friend of hers who's been to her house many times for dinner parties
Who she's shared so much of her life
Her career with
Who was there cooing at her son three days after his birth
And
Maybe it's the midday wine
Or a sudden inner capitulation
She looks down at the spoils of their lunch
And up at her colleague and the restaurant behind him
At the streetscape beyond
And life happening
And finally her colleague says
'Oh fuck.'
And 'Oh no.'
And 'Why are you crying?'

And Lauren has to smile and wipe tears away quickly and make something up.

Shift.

When Lauren gets home she drops her bag and coat in the front hallway and sits down in her home office.
She lifts the top of her laptop
And she opens the Andrew-Brittany audio files
And then she sees herself
At seventeen years old
Wandering the airport in Delaware
A distant cousin
Second or third but still for various reasons
Friendships within the family
This cousin was close with her aunt and her mother
And all of the joint family members think it's so kind that he's taking an interest in his young cousin.
Lauren's cousin
Dean
Had offered to have her come and stay for a couple of days with him in
Delaware
So they could have what was in those days called 'quality time' together.
Dean was in his thirties
An engineer
Owned a small landscaping business
Which
At the time
Lauren childishly thought involved clipping shrubs into shapes
But in fact involved cement trucks
And Dean
Sitting in an office in a managerial role
Hiring
Overseeing.
And that night when Lauren had showed up at the small Delaware airport
He'd been standing with a big sign that read

Cousin Lauren.
When he'd seen her he'd grinned and hugged her
And he'd given her
Lollipops
As a joke?
Or?
She'd unwrapped one
In his car on the drive from the airport
And yes and this was
He'd glanced over at her a few times while he was driving.
She could remember a sense of his amusement but also
Interest in her
And she knew?
Did she know what sucking on a lollipop might mean to him?
And of looking sideways at him while she did it?
During the car ride they'd talked about Dean's health because
Dean had had bladder cancer the previous year.
All the background family chatter all year had been about him
His chemo
His mood
The prognosis for bladder cancer
Schedules of those family members in Delaware
Who was going with him to chemo
Who was sitting with him as he threw up
Who was making his meals
Who was feeding his dog.
Dean
Was attractive
A little hollowed-out by the cancer but that square-jawed
American handsomeness.
They'd gone to a bar that night
Her small suitcase in the trunk of his car
And he'd bought her drinks
Which at seventeen felt adult
To be at a bar with a pint in front of her.
Not the drinking itself

She'd drunk a lot at house parties
But to be sitting and talking over beers
Men playing darts in the background.
Later that night
She'd brushed her teeth in Dean's bathroom
Smearing toothpaste on her toothbrush drunkenly
Then she'd fallen asleep in the spare bed.
In the middle of the night she'd woken up and as she woke up she understood that
That what was waking her up was
Dean
On top of her body
Kissing her
And
Once she understood it was real
She was able to unclench her body
Which felt rigid and Dean
Was murmuring things to her
That her lips were
So red
Like fruit
That there was a quality to her skin
That
Made him know
He was on the other side of cancer
How he felt more than ever now he had to grab ahold of things, of life
And as they kissed and fumbled he told her he loved her
And
Here she
Did he mean as her cousin?
Could he mean the other…?
Or both in some way she couldn't?
That wasn't accounted for in how she
Thought about
Love?
And all through this Dean seemed as though this is normal
An anticipated outcome of Lauren coming to his house
Like of course this is what should be happening now and

Maybe because Dean seems so normal
And is acting like this is normal
And his voice is normal and he laughs in his normal way
She finds she is able to say to him
'No, not sex, I can't, I have my period.'
And all through she keeps thinking
'I'm sure he thinks this is fine.'
'I'm sure he can't tell.'
Because while all this is happening she is so grossed out
By his cancer scar and by how hairy he is compared to the boys she's used to
By how adult even his desires seem as he shows her how to give him head
There is no embarrassment at talking her through what to do
And he's so confident as though this is routine for him to be doing something sexual when for the boys she knows sexuality is still more defined by newness than it is by pleasure
And the bodies of the boys are smooth and skinny and hairless and something frightens her about Dean's body
Its roughness
It doesn't smell like the boys she knows
Like sample cologne
It smells like sweet sweat
And for Lauren there is no sexuality in this.
She is not turned on but only too alert
As though she is painfully trying not to let him know how sickened she is
And she can't work out why she can't stop it
She cannot work out how to say no.
She does not once
Not once
Say no.
She doesn't say no.
She doesn't.
And by now it's light outside
And there are almost no thoughts in her head because
To have a thought would be too
And Dean smiles down at her

And gets out of bed to run her a bath.

LAUREN *wipes her lipstick off.*

As soon as Dean leaves her alone in the bathroom she takes out her tampon
Drops it in the toilet
It's so heavy with blood it makes a wet thud
And then she gets right in the bath.
Long minutes she sits there
Head down in silence.
As the bathtub fills up with blood
She is thinking:
This is terrible.
This
Is terrible
Because soon I'm going to
Go
Out of this room and into the house and into the world and how am I going to do that?

Shift.

An hour later
Dean drove her to her aunt's house
And Lauren had breakfast with him and her aunt.
Lauren remembers looking down at the eggs and toast and thinking how weird it was that they were all sitting having breakfast like a family.
It felt like she couldn't get hold of
What had even
Happened in
Reality.
It was almost as though nothing *had happened.*
It seemed so improbable.
Sitting there joking and laughing with Dean and her aunt all the normal ways conversations flowed
Which family dogs had died
Who had got into what colleges
And then a sudden upward glimpse of Dean's torso
His head thrown back

His hands in her hair
And then
'Was she looking forward to her last year of high school?'
She felt almost as though for the last twelve hours she'd been cold and warmth was returning to her and breakfast was happening in a hyperreal granular way
The taste of the eggs
The taste of the juice.
Dean and her aunt both had coffee.
She wasn't offered coffee because she was seventeen years old.
She drank her juice
And a few years later she told a college friend.
She downplayed it probably and the college friend laughed and said
'Oh fuck
The things that happen in your teens'
And rolled her eyes
And Lauren thinks, 'Yes'
'Okay'
'Good'
'That's what I thought.'
And she doesn't talk about it again for another fifteen years.

LAUREN *gets up and walks around to the back of her chair.*

LUKE *turns and looks at* LAUREN.

Who is standing somewhere on stage. He's again checking with her.

LAUREN. I'm just not sure what

What to
Yeah
No
Sorry
I'm sorry
Go on.

LUKE. Yeah?

LAUREN. Yeah

    I'm about to ask the question that's already in what I wrote.
    I'm yeah
    Getting ahead of myself.
    Sorry.

LUKE. Of course.

    No problem.

    LUKE *returns to the text.*

    In college
    When Lauren'd lived in that place in Montreal that was so romantic
    A walk-up apartment with high vaulted ceilings in that style that was so cheap and so plentiful in Montreal back then
    And that boyfriend
    Who wasn't a boyfriend yet
    Just a crush
    Somehow
    He'd figured out she had a crush on him
    And on a school trip
    To New York City to the opera
    They'd sat on the Greyhound bus
    Glancing at each other every few minutes.
    The Greyhound had pulled up at a gas station for a pit stop
    And he'd
    Taken her by the hand
    Walked her behind the gas station and the fast-food joints
    To a bank of payphones
    Pushed her body against it
    His knee between her legs
    Kissed her as hard as he could
    While classmates
    Came and went getting Tim Hortons in the background.
    And then he'd let go of her and they'd rejoined the throng
    And she'd gotten back on the bus
    And sat down
    Beside some girl who also liked opera

The bus jolting her
And jolting her
And Lauren had to
Breathe so as not to cum.
And back in Montreal
He'd found her on campus
Asked himself over
And they'd drunk the wine they could afford from the local depanneur
And they'd fucked
And
Fallen asleep
And she'd woken up at two a.m. to
Him
On top of her
Kissing her
Pushing her legs open
And
Half-in and out of sleep they'd fucked like that four times
And each time
She'd woken up at some point before the sex but not long before the sex.
With him
She'd liked that
And what in the end was the difference?
And also
How is it different than that time
She got drunk and
Did a couple of bumps of coke
And it seemed like a good idea
To fuck the
Sous chef
At the restaurant where she was working
And
She
Took him home
And as soon as he was inside her
Even as
They were still fucking

Even as it felt good
She regretted it and felt the beginnings of self-disgust.
Because the sous chef was
Only moderately attractive
And as he talked to her while fucking her she knew he was not a very interesting person
And she'd
Because of the coke
And the good lighting at the restaurant
Miscalculated
And now she
Wanted him gone
Out of her body
Out of her room
And wasn't that
Isn't that?
What in the end is the difference between that sous chef and her cousin?
The worst of it was she had sex she didn't want or regretted
Or what do you call sex that you are regretting as you are having it?
All you can do is think to yourself
As cheerfully as you can
Well that was terrible!
And move on.

LAUREN *moves toward* LUKE *and stands near him, as if about to ask a question.*

LUKE *turns and looks at* LAUREN.

LAUREN. I mean

Yeah
That's my question.
What's the difference?

LUKE. Uh

The difference between your cousin and the sous chef?

LAUREN. Yeah.

LUKE. Uh

>Okay
>Yeah I can
>Okay!
>I can try to answer that.

>*Beat.*

>LUKE *considers.*

>Okay well so with your cousin

>He comes into the spare bedroom where you're staying at his house in the middle of the night?

LAUREN. Yeah.

LUKE. And what's he wearing?

LAUREN. He's not wearing anything.

>*Beat.*

LUKE. He

>He comes into your room naked?

LAUREN. I mean I don't know because I don't know where he took his clothes off –

LUKE. But when you woke up he wasn't wearing any?

LAUREN. No.

LUKE. Okay.
Okay so
While you were asleep he got undressed
And then for a while he was on top of you touching you before you woke up?

LAUREN. I don't think that long –

LUKE. And – okay –

>And when you woke up was he turned on?

>LAUREN *looks at* LUKE.

>He was?

LAUREN *looks away.*

Okay cool

Cool.

Beat.

I think it's pretty clear what happened.
And I think it's clear why it's different for your cousin who shouldn't a) fuck his cousin and b) fuck his much younger cousin and c) come into his much younger cousin's bed in the middle of the night and start having sex with her while she's not awake so that by the time she wakes up he's jumped over the whole part where she can say yes or no.
I don't think starting to have sex with someone –
Anyone
Especially a seventeen-year-old family member –
When they're not awake is
Okay?

Beat.

And to answer your question yeah I think that's different than a boyfriend who you already had sex with that night making an assumption in the middle of the night that you might like more sex with him.

And I don't think that's the same as the sous chef who you wanted to have sex with at least until you didn't want to any more because you did at one point want to.
And with your cousin that wasn't the case.

LAUREN. But does he know it's different?

LUKE. Who?

Dean?

LAUREN. Especially because I didn't say no.

LUKE. Yeah

No
I think he knows.

LAUREN. But what was he thinking during all of that?
  Wasn't he thinking
  'I'm handsome
  She's pretty
  She ate those lollipops and she kept looking at me while she was eating them
  I'll teach her something about sex
  I'm an attractive older man
  She's going to have a nice time with me
  She came to my house
  She came to spend the night at my house
  What did she think was going to happen?'
  Something like that?

LUKE. Sure
  Maybe
  Whatever he was thinking
  Whatever it was
  He wasn't thinking about you.

  Beat.

LAUREN. Yeah.

  Beat.

  Okay but
  Isn't it true that
  So many fucked-up things happen when you're a teenager?
  I have so many.
  There were these boys in the parking lot at 7-Eleven.
  I was going to buy candy and they tried to pull my dress up
  And like I had to
  Run away from them.
  I was maybe thirteen.
  They had to be nineteen or twenty.
  There are so many of those things that happened.
  I mean isn't it just normal?

  Beat.

LUKE. I
 Yeah
 I
 What you're saying doesn't convince me it's normal.
 It convinces me that a lot of fucked-up things happened to you?

LAUREN. Yeah but that's the problem
 I just feel like if I got frustrated by every one of them
 Sure it was bad or could have been better or shouldn't have happened
 Maybe that's true
 But it feels in poor taste to go on and on about it…

LUKE. …I yeah…

LAUREN. …Like I'm trying to draw attention to myself

 Like I want everyone to feel sorry for me…

LUKE. I mean
 Maybe it's not that you want to talk about it all the time or draw attention to yourself
 Maybe you just don't want radio silence?

LAUREN. So it doesn't make you feel embarrassed when I talk about this
 Because you seem embarrassed.

LUKE. I am embarrassed but I don't know if
 That matters?

LAUREN. It does matter because I don't want to go around making people feel embarrassed all the time.
 I have to live with myself.
 And on top of which the whole thing's messy in my mind.
 I can hold on to it for a little that it shouldn't have happened or it was just on the wrong side of being okay or borderline something and then that goes away
 And even saying this out loud I know I sound
 Weak or

 Fucked up

Which is not who I am normally.
If you met me professionally I'd seem like a different person
I'd seem professional
And why struggle to articulate something that no one wants to hear anyway
That makes me feel stupid and sound confused
And that I don't even think is
Or can't place as being definitively one thing or another –

LUKE. I mean okay
I mean look
Yes to all that except the last part.
Because
Having to endure sex with a family member isn't maybe the best way to kick off a normal sex life.
And to figure out how to tell the difference between good sex and bad sex and wrong sex.

LAUREN looks at him.

Then looks away.

Pause.

LAUREN. Yeah.

Beat.

Yeah.

LUKE. Should I

Should I keep going?

LAUREN. Yeah.

LUKE returns to the text.

LUKE. Since that night with Dean
Lauren hasn't seen him.
He lives in Delaware
It's not that hard to avoid people who live in Delaware.
Dean
Sometimes contacts her on social media.
She doesn't answer

Mostly because she's confused about what to say
She's confused by her own desire to
Pretend it
Didn't happen and to be his cousin and have her aunts be her aunts.
She doesn't want to mess up all that and for what?
So that every holiday will be terrible?
So that the family will be uncomfortable
Truly uncomfortable
So that rifts will form between her mother and her aunts?
She's
And this is
The worst of it
Scared that if she does
See Dean
She'll be happy to see him
Because
Didn't he also when she was a little girl
Take her to the fair and win a massive cheap teddy bear for her that she treasured and that sat in the corner of her room for six or seven years slowly losing its stuffing?
And that part of their
Life
Their relationship
Is as strong
As that one night
Not enough maybe to totally obliterate it but
He's her cousin.
She can't just
Pretend he isn't.

Beat.

The next day
Lauren winds her way down the long institutional corridors at CAMH to sit with the group of women in the dingy room.
She
Sits
Listens to the women
Who

Have a new set of
Cautious observations about their poor circumstances.
This one
Is losing her looks and with them her confidence and how is she going to convince anyone to enter into a romance with a faded blonde with self-loathing issues?
That one
Has a boss who's always got a tone of surprise when she does good work and makes high-handed statements like
'This press release was actually very well executed, Alice?!'
And what does that mean for her promotion track?
Lauren
Listens to the therapist tell them how to combat their maladaptive thinking
How not to catastrophise.
How things are not as bad as the women think they are.
At the end of the session
A couple of the women wander down the sidewalk together
In the dirt and the noise of Toronto
Still talking
Animated
And into a coffee shop.
Lauren sits with them
And enjoys their ironic and thoughtful advice.
She feels
As she listens
She slips in and out of feelings of intense liking for them intermixed with disgust
Which
And then after a while the conversation swirls downward into the depths and she
Finds herself talking about
At first laughing but then talking openly
About
Her cousin
Dean.

Beat.

The women look back at her

Without shame
Without pity
Without a sudden stiffening that can happen when you admit to something uncomfortable like this
Without laughing it off.
No one tries to calibrate their reaction and say the right words
No one jokes to alleviate their discomfort
None of that.
They are
Considering her
Carefully
Quietly
Until the woman named Alice says
'I don't know what the category is for that
I think you get to choose
But
Here's what's familiar about what you said.
I do feel like there's a
Voice
The voice of
I don't know
All of us
And it's saying:
"Sh
It's fine.
Shhhhh
You're fine.
It'll be over in a minute
It'll be fine
Just get through it
It's not that big a deal
Shhhhhh."'
And the other women from the group
Lean in a little
As if to say
Yes
That is how it is
That's how it is.

And then one of the women says so quietly it's almost not said
'I'm sorry.'

Beat.

Later Lauren sits at her desk
Typing up the story about Andrew and Brittany
Putting it into sentences and paragraphs.
Her phone rings
And it's a number that's probably
Because of the area code
Going to be someone who's connected to the Andrew and Brittany article
When Lauren picks up she immediately recognises the voice as Brittany's.
Lauren goes still
Waits.
Brittany says
Cautiously
'Do you have a minute?'
And Lauren says
'Yes.'
There's a pause on the line and then Brittany says
'I have one thing to add
Would it be okay to add it?'
And Lauren says
'Yes of course.'
And Brittany says
'I should have admitted to you on the phone that I drink too much.
And that a lot of my memories from that night are blurry.
My lawyer told me not to say that.
But
I want you to know that I don't know what happened and
I may not be the best witness to my own story.'
Lauren, who is sitting there
Rigid
Unclenches and nods and says
'Yes of course.'

And 'Thank you.'
And then Lauren finds her voice again and asks
'What do you think happened to you that night?'
And Brittany says
Very softly
'I don't
I just
I don't know.'

Shift.

Epilogue

LUKE *turns to* LAUREN.

LUKE. And that's it
   That's all of it.

   LAUREN *nods.*

LAUREN. Yeah.

   LAUREN *exhales.*

   Beat.

   LAUREN *turns to the audience.*

   That's it.
   That's the end.
   So
   Thank you.

   LAUREN *turns to* LUKE.

   Thank you
   Luke.

LUKE. I uh
   Yeah

   Beat.

   I have to admit
   That uh
   That I
   That I'm
   Before we go
   Before they go
   Can I ask you something?

LAUREN. Yeah.

LUKE. Why did you want me to say all this for you?
   Why didn't you say it yourself?
   I'm wondering it.
   I think some of them might be wondering it too.

LUKE gestures to the audience.

   I
   To be honest
   I think some of them might be uncomfortable about a man saying it all for you
   Although I also think some of them probably didn't notice that there's anything to notice about me saying it for you…

Then LAUREN pauses, considers.

   Maybe you don't know the answer…
   Maybe you don't know what I'm asking…

LAUREN. Uh
   No I do
   Uh so because I'm a journalist I wrote it all down
   And then lately I wanted to hear the whole thing in front of

LAUREN gestures to the audience.

   People
   And I wanted a voice that was
   Neutral and steady
   And had authority
   That's believable
   To tell it.
   So that I could maybe better figure out what to think about it all.

LAUREN thinks about what she just said.

She swallows down emotion.

   Which…?
   Yeah
   I mean yeah.
   I mean
   Hunh.

Beat.

Does that…?

LUKE. Yeah no that's clear
 I get it uh
 Yeah
 And uh
 How was that?

LAUREN *considers him for as long as she wants.*

LAUREN. Yeah
 It was good.
 It helped.
 I feel
 Clearer
 Than I have
 But uh
 I guess
 I guess
 I could have been the one to tell it
 Well
 Doesn't matter
 Does it?
 I feel better.

LAUREN *considers* LUKE.

LUKE *considers* LAUREN.

LUKE. You feel better?

LAUREN. I do.
 I feel better.

Slowly, slowly, slowly, LAUREN *turns to the audience.*

 It helped.
 You
 You helped.
 Thank you.

End play.

Acknowledgements

The author would like to thank the Canada Council for the Arts, Dalhousie University, Soulpepper Theatre Company, the Luminato Festival, and, above all, 2b theatre company for the development of this work.

www.nickhernbooks.co.uk

@nickhernbooks